BEAUTIFUL

BONSAI

Text: Colin Lewis
Photography: Neil Sutherland
Illustrations: Tim Heyward, courtesy of Bernard Thornton Artists
Editorial: Laura Potts
Design: Amanda Sedge
Director of Production: Gerald Hughes

Author's Acknowledgements
A bonsai is a work of art, whose beauty is entirely dependent upon the skills of
its current caretaker. It is therefore important to record who is responsible for the
beauty of the specimen bonsai pictured in this book. I am particularly grateful to
my friends Peter Chan, of Herons Nursery, whose specimens appear on pages 7
and 33, and Ruth Stafford-Jones whose specimens appear on the back cover and
page 5. The tree featured on the front cover and all the other trees featured are
from my own collection.

CLB 4327
Published by Grange Books
an imprint of Grange Books PLC,
The Grange, Grange Yard, London SE1 3AG.
© 1995 CLB Publishing
Godalming, Surrey, England.
All rights reserved.
Printed and bound in Singapore.
Published in 1995
ISBN 1-85627-620-1

BEAUTIFUL

BONSAI

Grange
BOOKS

INTRODUCTION

A bonsai – which translated literally from Japanese means 'a tree in a pot' – is not a naturally dwarfed tree, neither is it treated with any special potion or chemical to stop it growing larger. Its growth is not restricted by confining the roots in a pot, but by constant clipping and trimming. The size and shape are entirely determined by its keeper whose horticultural and artistic skills also determine its eventual health and aesthetic quality. The skills of the bonsai artist have long been admired in the West and many people yearn to learn the techniques needed to create these magnificent living works of art. This introduction to the ancient art of bonsai concentrates on transforming garden centre stock into bonsai.

BUYING GUIDE

Try to buy the plant during the summer when you can be sure that it is in its growing season. If you do buy a plant in the winter ensure that you scrape back a little of the bark to make sure that the wood underneath is still green. As a general rule of thumb avoid slow growing or dwarf varieties for bonsai as they can take a long time to respond to training. If you want a flowering species choose one which flowers on the previous year's wood. This is important, as if the blooms are borne on current year's growth the shoots will need to grow disproportionately long before flowering begins. Always test the branches to check that they are supple enough to be shaped by wiring. Finally, decide on a variety which already has smallish leaves or needles and shows a readiness to produce buds on older wood. Before you buy a plant, carry out the following checks to ensure that you buy the plant with the most potential.

Roots

Good surface roots are essential in bonsai. Brush away a little of the soil to expose the surface roots of the plant to see if they appear natural, as unusual root formations will be difficult to work with.

Trunk

Remember that in bonsai the existing trunk line will not necessarily be the final one and the new bonsai does not have to be the same size as the raw material. There is no need, therefore, to buy a plant with an unusual trunk line. Indeed, as unusual often means unnatural, these plants will not make good bonsai. It is also important to avoid plants that have been grafted onto sturdier root stocks, as where the tree is grafted there is often an unsightly swelling which gets worse as the tree ages.

Branches

Make sure that the plant has plenty of branches which still bear foliage close to the trunk. This will present you with many possibilities when you get home and begin to design your bonsai.

General Health

Check that the tree is firm in its pot. Avoid any plants that have die back, as this may be the symptom of disease. Make sure that the soil is loose and porous, moist but not waterlogged and ensure that there is not an excessive growth of weeds in the pot, as this can be a symptom of poor quality soil and drainage.

HOW A BONSAI GROWS

In order to create successful bonsai it is vital to have an understanding of how the different parts of a tree function.

Roots
The roots of a tree perform three functions. They hold the tree steady in the soil, they store nutrients during the dormant period and they absorb water and nutrients through root hairs. Care should be taken not to overfeed the tree, as this may result in root rot, a decay that results in a yellowing or wilting of the leaves.

Trunk and Branches
Like the roots, the trunk acts as a support for the tree and is used to store nutrients. More importantly, it is used to carry water and nutrients from one part of the tree to another. This takes place in tissue located either side of the cambium layer – a single-cell layer, located just beneath the bark. The sapwood, or xylem, situated on the inside of the cambium layer, is the means by which water is transported from the roots to all parts of the tree. The outside layer of tissue, the phloem, is responsible for distributing the sugars produced in the leaves to other parts of the tree. During the growing season the cambium layer produces a new layer of both xylem and phloem. The cambium layer is also responsible for controlling growth, producing new roots in cuttings and air layers, as well as the tissue to heal over wounds.

Foliage

Leaves convert water supplied by the roots and carbon dioxide absorbed from the air into sugars that provide growth energy to the plant. During the day the leaves 'breathe in' through small pores called stomata and at night they expel the excess oxygen and other gaseous by-products. Water also evaporates through the surface of the leaves.

Buds

Buds contain an entire new shoot, minutely formed within a protective sheath of scales. Terminal or apical buds, formed at the tips of the current year's shoots, contain the next year's extension growth. Axillary buds are formed along the length of the shoot, in each leaf axil (the point where the leaf stem, or petiole, joins the shoot), or in the axils of the bud scales. They will either produce the shorter side shoots next year or remain dormant. Dormant buds are generally axillary buds which failed to open in the year following their formation. Adventitious buds can emerge anywhere on old wood, particularly around pruning cuts, and are generally the tree's response to improved conditions.

𝔼QUIPMENT

𝕰ℭ

All you really need in the way of equipment for your first attempts at growing bonsai are a pair of sharp scissors, wire cutters, a pair of bypass secateurs, nail scissors for fine work and a pointed steel hook for combing out roots. As you gain experience, however, you may begin to find these tools clumsy and inadequate. Certainly, sooner or later you will want to invest in your first proper bonsai tools.

Scissors are the cheapest tools to buy and as such make a good first purchase. Long scissors for trimming and short shears for heavier work such as root pruning will prove to be invaluable.

Side cutters which can cut branches cleanly and accurately, and some long-handled wire cutters, designed to cut right up to the tip should come next.

Curved branch cutters used for pruning close to the trunk, where a slight hollow is required to help the wound heal over

quickly, and bonsai pliers, which are useful for stripping jins, as well as for manipulating the wire once it has been applied to the tree, will complete the set of essential bonsai tools.

All the other tools are more specialist in their application and can be bought as and when the need arises. It is important to keep your tools sharp by honing them on a fine, oiled, sharpening stone, and sterilising them after use by immersing them in methylated spirit.

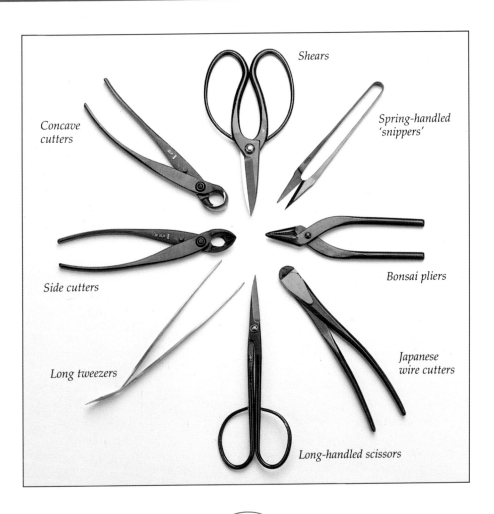

Shears

Spring-handled 'snippers'

Concave cutters

Bonsai pliers

Side cutters

Japanese wire cutters

Long tweezers

Long-handled scissors

POTS

A bonsai pot is an integral part of the composition and must complement the tree, the two forming a harmonious unit. As well as the aesthetic considerations the pot also has to satisfy some practical requirements.

1. The pot must be stoneware, which is frost-proof, as opposed to earthenware, which is not. A simple test is to wet the *unglazed surface of the pot to see if it absorbs the water. If it does it is earthenware, while if the water wipes off*

cleanly the pot is stoneware.

2. The pot must have adequate drainage. The holes should be at least three times greater in number and size than in a conventional flower pot.

3. The floor of the pot must be level, so that no pockets of water can accumulate in the base. Check that there are no indentations in the corners where the feet are fixed. It is important that the pot has feet in order for there to be space for the drained water to flow away.

4. Pots that are glazed on the inside should be avoided, as the glaze is an inhospitable surface for the roots and will cause the soil to dry out too quickly around the perimeter of the pot.

Pots made of mica are now sold by a number of nurseries and retail at less than half the price of stoneware pots. These are ideal for temporary or training pots, but as the surface scratches easily they are unsuitable for exhibiting.

ROOT PRUNING

As a tree matures in the wild some older roots die back and are replaced by strong new ones that do most of the work, absorbing water and nutrients. In a pot this cycle has to be recreated artificially in order to keep your bonsai healthy. A healthy young bonsai – say up to ten years old – will need to be root pruned each year. Older trees, however, need to be pruned less often, perhaps every five years. The best time to root prune is in the spring, just as the roots begin to grow. The first sign of root activity is a slight swelling of the buds on last year's shoots. To check further, gently lift the tree from its pot and look closely at the roots. If the tips appear to be swelling the time is right. If the tips are white they have already started to grow but pruning will do them no harm so long as the new buds have not opened yet.

1. The roots of this medium-sized trident maple are filling the pot and need to be pruned. They are all healthy, and as you can see, they have already started to grow.

2. Lift the tree from its pot and carefully comb out the roots, working from the centre outwards.

3. Comb out the underneath of the root mass, being careful not to tear the roots. When you have finished you should have removed about a third of the total volume of soil.

4. Use a sharp pair of scissors to trim the roots back so that the remaining root mass doesn't quite fill the pot. It is important to trim the roots underneath as well, otherwise the tree will rise in its pot as it grows.

REPOTTING

Once the roots of your bonsai have been pruned it should
be repotted. You can repot the tree in the same container, or
in one that is more suitable.

1. First cover the drainage holes with
mesh. Then push the wire through the
mesh and drainage holes and bend the legs
up tight against the underneath of the pot.

2. Some pots have additional small holes
for tie wires. If not, you can use the

drainage holes. You need at least two
pieces of wire to make the tree secure until
the roots have re-established.

3. Cover the floor of the pot with coarse
grit to aid drainage. If the pot is less than
an inch deep you do not need a drainage
course, provided the soil is sufficiently free-
draining. Cover the grit with a layer of
fresh soil. Make a small mound of soil
where the trunk will sit.

4. Take the pruned tree and nestle it into the mound of soil, with the surface of the root mass just below the pot's rim. Then pull the wire ties down over the root mass as illustrated and twist them together until the tree does not rock. Cushion the bark with squares of rubber or foam to protect it.

5. Fill the remaining spaces with fresh, dry soil. Work the soil in between the roots using the fingers, ensuring that there are no air pockets. Water the newly potted tree well, but use a fine rose or spray, so that you don't wash away the new soil. Repeat the operation a few minutes later to ensure a thorough soaking.

Shaping With Wire

ℰᗰ ᘓℬ

Wire of a suitable gauge is coiled around a branch or shoot and the two are then manoeuvred into the desired position. After a period of growth, the branch will be set in that position and the wire can be removed. For some species this may take a couple of years, for others it may only take a couple of weeks. Older, stiffer branches, should be bent little by little every few weeks until the desired position is achieved.

1. Hold the wired part of the branch firmly with one hand and coil the wire with the other. The wire coils should be at approximately 45 degrees. If the coils are too close together it reduces the holding power and restricts the flow of sap, if they are too far apart there will not be enough holding power.

2. Spread your hands on the branch so that you hold as much of it as possible. Gradually bend the branch, using both thumbs as leverage points. Once bent, the wire should hold the branch in position. If the branch springs back, the wire is too thin, if it cuts the bark, it is too tight.

3

4

3. When wiring long branches, reduce the thickness of the wire as the branch diameter decreases. Overlap the different thicknesses by two or three turns.

4. When wiring a side branch, anchor the wire by coiling it around the trunk. Always take it through the fork of the branch as shown. Use one piece of wire for two branches, as this provides perfect anchorage. Coil the wire in opposite directions on each branch, to prevent it uncoiling as you work.

REMOVING WIRE

Bonsai wire, which is available in a wide variety of gauges and subdued colours, is easy to work with. The sheer ease of manipulation makes it a joy to use and justifies the extra expense.

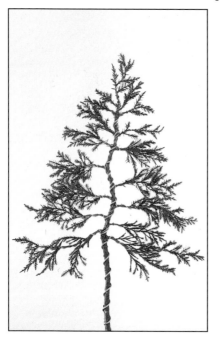

It is important to avoid the temptation of unwinding the wire once it has served its purpose, in order to use it another time, as it is much easier to damage the bark, or even snap the branch when working in reverse. The branch will have swollen so the wire will be tighter than when you first applied it and will naturally be full of kinks, making it difficult to manipulate. The best way to remove the wire is to cut it off. Custom-made Japanese bonsai wire cutters are designed for this purpose but can be quite expensive. To start with, good quality electrical wire cutters, preferably with long handles to enable you to reach awkward places, will do the job just as well. Any damage to the bark caused by the cutters will be superficial and will heal much quicker than damage caused by careless uncoiling.

BRANCH PRUNING

When pruning branches great care should be taken to minimise the risk of unsightly swellings around the wound and to encourage the scar to blend in with the character of the trunk. When pruning branches always use very sharp tools, that have been sterilised by immersing them in methylated spirit for a few minutes. Once you have made the cut, make sure that the cambium layer (located between bark and heartwood) is properly sealed. If left exposed it may die back, increasing the size of the wound and delaying the healing process. Feed the tree well after drastic pruning, to speed up the healing process, and make sure that any unwanted shoots which arise from around the wound are rubbed off as soon as they appear.

1. Use a pair of 'bypass' secateurs to cut off the branch, making sure that the non-cutting blade is furthest from the trunk. Leave a small stub at first, rather than attempting to cut right up to the trunk.

2. If you do have special branch pruners, use them to finish off the cut as close to the trunk as possible. The wound will heal more neatly if you create a slight hollow in the exposed wood.

3. Clean up the edges of the wound with a very sharp knife. Ragged edges heal unevenly and are likely to harbour fungal spores which can infect the whole tree.

4. Seal the wound thoroughly, especially around the edges, with bonsai sealant. A little olive oil mixed with grafting wax or children's modelling clay can be used as a substitute.

Maintenance Pruning

Each year your bonsai will throw out new shoots from the buds created in the leaf axils during the previous growing season. In a semi-mature bonsai these shoots should be allowed to grow to six or seven leaves before they are cut back. Allowing a period of free growth thickens the parent branches and trunk. New shoots will emerge from the buds in the remaining leaf axils. In an established bonsai, however, this annual growth will need to be cut back during the dormant season to allow the next season's growth room to extend before outgrowing the design. Over the seasons this constant 'clip-and-grow' technique will reward you with a branch structure with all the characteristics of an ancient tree. These steps look at branch pruning a maple.

1. Cut back the long shoots produced in the previous growing season to a short shoot or a spur.

2. Every few years, prune away older growth to prevent overcrowding and to maintain neat foliage pads.

3. Finally, cut back all spurs to one or two buds, being careful to prune to a bud which points in the direction that you want the new growth to take. Look very carefully at the base of each spur as the buds can be minute.

4. The pruned branch might look rather naked, but every remaining bud will generate a new shoot next season, producing a more compact twig structure.

SUMMER PINCHING

Once a tracery of fine twigs has been built and refined, the resulting foliage pads must be kept trimmed and in balance with the design. This is achieved by pinching out the tips of all new growth as it appears. The following techniques describe how summer pinching should be carried out for the five most common growth patterns.

1. *Spruce buds open to form tiny, bright green tufts which should be plucked before they are fully elongated. Try to spread the job over a period of time.*

2. *As pine buds begin to grow they elongate forming 'candles' which should have up to two thirds snapped off before the needles develop. Twist and bend at the same time.*

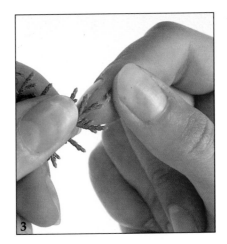

3. Junipers produce prolific new growth, which is distinguished by its lighter colour. Hold the fan of foliage in one hand and pull out all extending growth with the finger and thumb of the other.

4. Zelkovas and other alternate-leaved species produce new leaves one at a time at the shoot tips. This leaf, and the minute bud at its base, should be pinched out, using tweezers as necessary.

5. Maples produce new leaves in pairs borne on a short extending shoot. Both leaves should be pinched out, together with the tiny developing bud nestled between them.

CREATING A JIN

*J*ins – defined in bonsai terms as a dead branch that has shed its bark – occur naturally on most old conifers and on some deciduous trees. By artificially creating them on a bonsai you can impart a feeling of great age. The best time to create jins is during the summer, when the bark is full of sap and is easier to strip. For maximum effect, ensure that the size of the jin is in proportion to the size of the bonsai. It is important to remember that although jins do not grow, foliage masses do, so do not cut the jin too small at first.

1. To create a jin, make an eye-shaped cut in the bark around the base of the branch. Then make another cut along its length.

2. Squeezing the bark with some flat-jawed pliers helps separate the bark from the wood. This is especially effective during spring and summer when the sap is on the move.

3. Peel away the bark. A natural-looking shape and texture can be created by peeling back slivers of wood, exposing the grain. Jins look better if they are randomly formed rather than being carved. Remove any fuzz, with fine sandpaper, being careful not to make the jin perfectly smooth.
4. Treat the jin with lime sulphur, to bleach and preserve the wood. Lime sulphur smells foul, so work outside.

BROOM-STYLE ZELKOVA

The creation of this geometric branch structure requires a
precise, calculated approach. To be successful the plant
must have a trunk thickness anything from three-quarters
of an inch to four inches or more. This will make it easier to
execute the initial cut, so making it more likely for shoots to
be thrown out from the cambium layer exposed by the cut,
rather than from lower down the trunk.

*1. Tie the plant into its container to help
prevent too much strain on the roots
during cutting. Using a very sharp, fine
toothed saw, make two cuts to form an
unequal-sided, 'V'-shaped surface at the
required height.*

*2. Clean up any ragged edges with a sharp
knife and seal the entire cut surface with
bonsai sealant, especially around the edge,
where the cambium layer is located.
Within approximately six or seven weeks
new shoots should start to push through
the sealant.*

3. Tie some waterproof tape tightly around the emerging shoots to ensure that there is a smooth transition from trunk to branch without unsightly swelling.

4. By the time the shoots have reached this size they will be ready to prune. Cut the long shoots back to two or three leaves and thin out some of the weaker shoots as well. New shoots will grow from each leaf axil and they, too, will be shortened. This cycle will need to be repeated many times over.

This classic broom style, or hokidachi, zelkova would have taken up to ten years or more to develop its fine tracery of twigs.

Informal Upright Maple

It is possible to take advantage of the natural resilience of a tree that has been allowed to thicken to about half an inch, to create an informal upright style with severe taper. This Japanese maple is five years old and, like most trees of this age, it has retained two small, weak branches which mark the position of the end of the first season's growth. These become the new leader and the first major branch.

1

2

1. Wrap the roots to preserve moisture, then cut the trunk directly above the bottom two branches or dormant buds. The branch on the left is chosen to become the new leader and is pruned at the point where the next angle is planned, just above a pair of buds. Seal the large wound with bonsai sealant.

2. Shorten the long roots to promote a compact root structure and plant in a clay pot. Plant the tree at an angle so that one branch is horizontal, and the other, the new leader, points upwards at an angle. Water and feed well.

3. After a few weeks of vigorous growth, it is time to prune. Thin out the small shoots around the pruning scars, leaving a shoot for the second branch and one for the new

leader, as well as one at the rear to form the first back branch.

4. After another few weeks the maple is ready for its third prune. This leaves three side branches, one to the rear, and four sections of trunk. One more year and the structure will be complete.

CEDAR LITERATI STYLE

The Literati style was originally inspired by the brush strokes of ancient Chinese scribes. The essence of the design is the trunk line, which should have taper and should present many changes of direction. The branches are limited to the uppermost portion of the trunk and foliage is kept to a minimum. The attraction of this cedar was the long, lower branch. It became the new leader, so creating an ancient-looking and dramatic effect.

1. Cut away the elastic net around the roots and disentangle them.

2. Remove the unwanted upper trunk, leaving a stub to form a jin. Using a branch as the new leader increases taper and creates a sharp bend. Clean the short spurs and tufts of foliage from the trunk and the first quarter of each branch. Then select which branches are to be kept and which are to be pruned.

3. *Jin the stub of the original trunk (page 30/31) and wire the trunk and branches (page 20/21). When shaping, aim for a combination of sharp bends and gradual curves, remembering to work in three dimensions.*

4. *Having established the basic trunk and branch structure, the final tidying up takes place. Remove any downward facing buds or shoots.*

5. *Finally, wire the tree firmly into the pot to make sure that it is really secure.*

WINDSWEPT JUNIPER

ℴℴ

The success of this dramatic style depends on the potential of the raw material, so try to choose a plant which already has a tendency to grow towards one side. In nature, winds not only shape the branches, they also strip young shoots and only allow new growth at the tips, a process that the bonsai artist imitates following the initial styling. This will inevitably lead to over-extended growth, and every few years the foliage pads should be cut back and re-grown.

1. Wrap the root ball of a Chinese juniper in netting to keep it intact while you work. Start by removing all dead shoots and weak, spindly branches, working from underneath the main trunk line. Then, prune more branches, to create the effect of

a windswept tree that has retained just a few branches on the lee side.
2. Remove unwanted branches and jin some of the thicker ones (page 30/31). Hold the tree at the correct angle by an upturned pot.

3. Wire the remaining branches (page 20/21), so that they follow the wind-blown sweep of the trunk, with similar curves, but on a decreasing scale.

4. Cut off all downward-facing shoots to emphasise the flowing branch lines, characteristic of the windswept style. Then trim the foliage pads, making them into narrow wedge shapes.

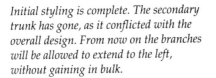

Initial styling is complete. The secondary trunk has gone, as it conflicted with the overall design. From now on the branches will be allowed to extend to the left, without gaining in bulk.

Scots Pine

This bonsai, which is relatively straight-trunked with cascading branches, imitates the way that pine trees tend to grow naturally in the West. Work should be carried out on the tree over a period of weeks, any time between early summer – when new needles are hardening off – and early autumn. For the best results do not repot the tree immediately after styling, but wait a year. The tree that has been chosen for this bonsai has a fork about halfway up the trunk, plenty of branches and a small secondary trunk.

1. Begin by removing the thickest fork. Prune all but one or two branches from each of the 'whorls' of branches that the pine produces, leaving only those that are needed for the design.

2. Mark the front – the part of the tree that displays the best trunk shape – with a pencil stuck in the pot. Then position the secondary trunk so it is visible from the front. Remove all old needles to make wiring easier and to encourage back budding, before wiring the lower left branch.

4a

3. The main branches are positioned to cascade gently from the trunk, curves are introduced to the upper trunk. The original leader is removed and replaced with a smaller branch.

4. Wires are not sufficient to hold the secondary trunk in place, so a tourniquet fixed to the pot's rim takes the strain. This can be tightened a little every few weeks if necessary.

5

5. After more thinning, the secondary branches are wired into position. Every shoot is then wired to face outwards or upwards to form domed pads.

4b

Watering Your Bonsai

ഇ൪ ൪ങ

In theory, provided your bonsai is growing in a free-draining soil, it should not be possible to over water. Yet many beginners, in their enthusiasm, manage to do just that. Over watering eliminates the air contained in the spaces between the soil particles and drowns the roots. It also creates the conditions favoured by various root rotting fungi. The symptoms of decaying roots (yellowing foliage and lack of new growth) are not usually apparent until the damage has already been done. Having said this, it does take a few weeks for the problem to become serious, so the odd drenching now and

then won't hurt. On the other hand it may only take twenty-four hours for a bonsai to die of thirst, so it is essential to prevent the soil drying out completely.

Generally, the best method is to water the surface of the soil evenly, using a fine rose or spray, until the water drains out of the drainage holes. Wait a few minutes and repeat. This ensures a thorough wetting of the soil and should be sufficient for one day during the height of summer. Try to avoid watering a tree that doesn't really need it. Wind can dry the soil's surface to a crisp, while deeper in the pot it may still be quite wet. If in doubt check by scraping away the surface in a couple of places and adjust the amount of water accordingly.

The best time to water is in early evening. This gives the tree plenty of time to have a good drink before morning. If you water in the morning the tree doesn't have much of a chance to refresh itself before the heat of the day. If you can't avoid watering in the morning do it as early as possible. Another advantage with evening watering is that you can douse the foliage at the same time without the risk of leaf scorch caused by the water droplets acting as miniature magnifying glasses in the sun. All bonsai appreciate a daily shower.

Don't assume that the rain will do the watering for you. A bonsai acts like an umbrella, and it shelters the pot from all but the heaviest downpour, so it is well worth continuing to check the need for water even in wet weather.

FEEDING YOUR BONSAI

There are three ways to apply fertiliser: by placing pellets on or in the soil, by watering it onto the soil and by spraying it on the leaves (foliar feeding).

Fertiliser Pellets
Specialist bonsai fertiliser pellets are available from all nurseries. They can be either the organic variety, such as rape seed cake, or

inorganic. Both types release nutrients slowly, which means that you don't have to worry about feeding for a while. The disadvantage of this type of feeding is that you can't adjust the pattern without risking over feeding.

Soil Application

Large numbers of soluble fertilisers are available, most of which are suitable for bonsai, though it is advisable not to use one that is specifically intended for house plants as it will tend to be too rich. Apply the fertiliser routinely once a week or at a quarter strength with every watering. Never use a stronger solution that the manufacturers state and try to change the brand occasionally in order to maintain a balanced diet. The main problem presented by soluble fertilisers is that the nutrients wash out of the soil quickly. Also, during very wet weather, you may not be able to feed your trees without the risk of over watering.

Foliar Feeding

Research has shown that a plant can absorb more nutrients through its leaves than through its roots. Many standard soluble fertilisers can be applied in this way, while some are specifically designed for this type of use. Foliar feeding is useful when your bonsai has root problems or when the soil is very wet. Foliar feeds are easy to apply provided you don't do so in strong sun, when the leaves may scorch. In warm, windy weather, however, the solution dries on the leaves too quickly and leaves a powdery deposit that is difficult to wash off.